F £13.95

C000132219

SAMUEL BARBER
Ten Selected Songs

ED 4400
First Printing: June 2008

ISBN 978-1-4234-3894-6

G. SCHIRMER, Inc.

DISTRIBUTED BY

 HAL•LEONARD®
CORPORATION
7777 W. BLUEMOUND RD. P.O. BOX 13819 MILWAUKEE, WI 53213

www.schirmer.com
www.halleonard.com

CD TRACK LIST

	Performance Track	Accompaniment Track
Mother, I cannot mind my wheel [1]*	1	11
Hey nonny no! [2]*	2	12
A Slumber Song of the Madonna [1]	3	13
Strings in the earth and air [2]	4	14
Bessie Bobtail [1]	5	15
With rue my heart is laden [2]	6	16
The Secrets of the Old [1]	7	17
The Crucifixion [1]	8	18
The Daisies [2]	9	19
Sure on this shining night [1]	10	20

Performers on the CD: [1] **Kathleen Sonnentag, mezzo-soprano**
[2] **Kurt Ollmann, baritone**
Richard Walters, piano

* world premiere recording

CONTENTS

First published in this edition

PREFACE

The ten songs in this collection were chosen not only for musical appeal, but also because of suitability for students of voice.

Samuel Barber (1910–1981) began composing at the age of seven, and in that same year wrote his first song. By the time he wrote "A Slumber Song of the Madonna" in 1925, the earliest song in this collection, he had composed 16 songs, 13 piano pieces, an expansive two-piano work, and a first opera, attempted at the age of ten. Between 1924 and 1936 Barber composed more than 50 songs. He was self-critical in the extreme, and as a result only seven songs from this period were published in his lifetime. Others were published posthumously in *Ten Early Songs* (G. Schirmer, 1994). *Ten Selected Songs* marks the first publication of two further early songs, both composed in 1927: "Mother, I cannot mind my wheel," and "Hey nonny no!"

Many of the earliest unpublished works are salon songs in style. Barber's more substantial art song style began to emerge organically, particularly influenced by American composer Sidney Homer (1864–1953), Barber's uncle and a model for the boy's composition, especially of art songs. Barber was greatly influenced by Homer's choice in poets. Contralto Louise Homer (1871–1947), a star at the Metropolitan Opera, was Sidney's wife and Barber's aunt. Barber often persuaded her to try out songs for him privately, and she sang a few early Barber songs on professional recitals.

Even in the most unsophisticated unpublished student work, Barber's gift for writing lyrically for the voice is apparent, as is his natural ability to set words to music. Even though sometimes short, all his early songs are complete compositional ideas.

Barber entered the newly founded Curtis Institute of Music in Philadelphia in 1924, where he was considered a genius by fellow students. Unusually, he had three primary areas of study: piano, voice (he was a lyric baritone), and composition/theory. Six of the ten songs in this collection were composed during his years at Curtis, where he studied composition until 1934. A fellow student of Barber's at Curtis and a regular singer of his songs was mezzo-soprano Rose Bampton, who went on to sing at the Metropolitan Opera. Barber also sang some of his early songs himself while a student at Curtis.

A Slumber Song of the Madonna
Originally composed for voice and organ in 1925, first performed by Louise Homer with the composer at the organ. She later performed the voice/piano version Barber made on a 1927 recital tour. This song remained unpublished during the composer's life, published posthumously in *Ten Early Songs*, in the key of F minor/A-flat Major, which is used in the High Voice edition of *Ten Selected Songs*. Its transposition down to E minor/G major makes its first appearance in the Low Voice edition of this collection.

Mother, I cannot mind my wheel
Hey nonny no!
Both songs were composed in 1927 when Barber was a student at Curtis. They receive their first publication in this edition, and also premiere recordings on the companion CDs. They may have had student performances at Curtis, but based on information available, subsequent professional performances were unlikely.

The manuscripts for both songs include no specific tempo indications, dynamics or articulations. The *ritardandos* and *a tempos* in "Hey nonny no!" are Barber's. Minimal editorial suggestions have been indicated in brackets. Decisions about tempo, dynamics and phrasing were made in recording the songs, but other interpretations and points of view are possible.

It is not difficult to imagine Barber studying Schubert songs such as "Gretchen am Spinnrade" at the age of 16 or 17, the time of composing "Mother, I cannot mind my wheel." The song is obviously reminiscent of the sentiments of Goethe's poem. Barber also uses a pianistic repetitive accompanying figure in Schubertian manner, an approach not common in his songs, which are more often aesthetically related to Schumann and Brahms.

"Hey nonny no!" (original key of C major) has a rowdy, boisterous spirit uncommon in Barber's music, an antidote to melancholy. It is not improbable that Barber himself sang this song as a student, since it seems suited to a baritone. This anonymous 16th century poem was available in various sources in 1927, one of which was *The Oxford Book of English Verse: 1250–1900*, published in 1919.

The Daisies
With rue my heart is laden
Both songs were composed in 1927. The composer designated them part of Three Songs, Op. 2, published by G. Schirmer in 1936. Barber dedicated "The Daisies" to his mother. "With rue my heart is laden" was dedicated to Gama Gilbert, a close Barber friend at Curtis.

Bessie Bobtail
Composed in 1934, but chosen by Barber to be published in Three Songs, Op. 2, it was dedicated to Edith and John Braun, marking the winter months of 1934 Barber spent with them in Vienna. Edith Evans Braun was a composer and pianist; John Braun was a singer. The original key, found in the High Voice edition of this collection, appears in both High and Low Voice editions of *Samuel Barber: Collected Songs*. The transposition down a whole step makes its first appearance in *Ten Selected Songs*.

Strings in the earth and air
Composed on December 3, 1935 as part of Four Songs, Op. 10, settings of poems from James Joyce's *Chamber Music*, it remained unpublished in Barber's lifetime; published posthumously in *Ten Early Songs*. It appears in its original key in the High Voice edition of *Ten Selected Songs*, transposed for the first time for the Low Voice edition.

The Secrets of the Old
Sure on this shining night
Both songs were composed in 1938 as part of Four Songs, Op. 13, premiered in 1941 by soprano Barbara Troxell, a student at Curtis from 1939 to 1942. Barber finally met James Agee, author of "Sure on this shining night," in 1948 when setting the Agee text for *Knoxville: Summer of 1915*. They were friends until Agee's death in 1955.

The Crucifixion
Barber composed the *Hermit Songs*, settings of medieval writings of monks, between October of 1952 and February of 1953. "The Crucifixion" was the first song composed of the cycle, on October 26, 1952. Soprano Leontyne Price had made a splash in *Porgy and Bess*, but had not yet made a recital debut. Barber considered her among other singers, including Dietrich Fischer-Dieskau, as the debut artist for *Hermit Songs*. Price and Barber premiered the cycle at Coolidge Auditorium at the Library of Congress, Washington, DC, on October 30, 1953. The original key of "The Crucifixion," found in the High Voice edition of this collection, appears in both High and Low Voice editions of *Samuel Barber: Collected Songs*. The transposition down a whole step makes its first appearance in *Ten Selected Songs*.

Richard Walters
editor
June, 2008

to Edith and John Braun

Bessie Bobtail
original key: D minor

James Stephens*

Samuel Barber
Op. 2, No. 3

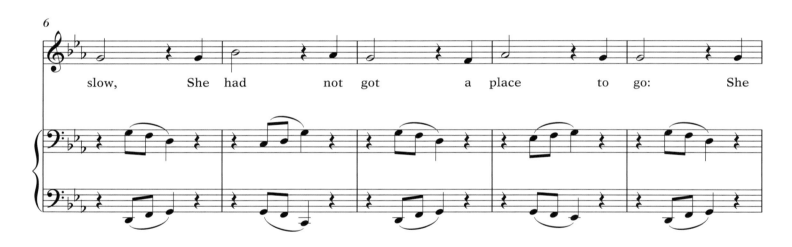

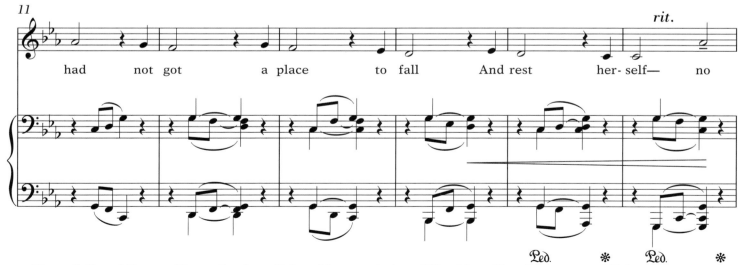

*From *Collected Poems of James Stephens.* Printed by permission of The Macmillan Company, publishers.

place at all! She stumped a - long, and wagged her pate; And said a thing was des - per - ate. Her face was screwed and wrin-kled tight Just like a nut— and, left and right, On ei - ther side, she wagged her head And

The Crucifixion
from *Hermit Songs*
original key: A minor

From The Speckled Book, 12th century
Translated by Howard Mumford Jones*

Samuel Barber
Op. 29, No. 5

*From *Romanesque Lyric,* by permission of the University of North Carolina Press.

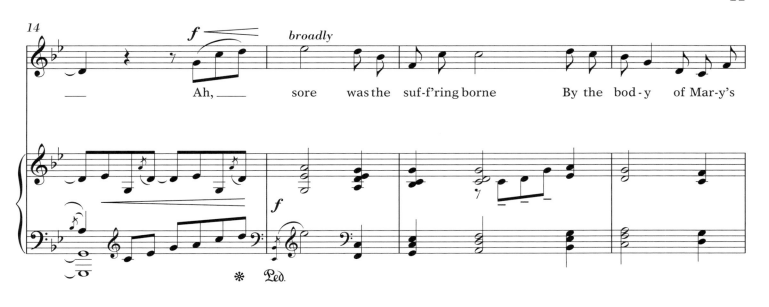

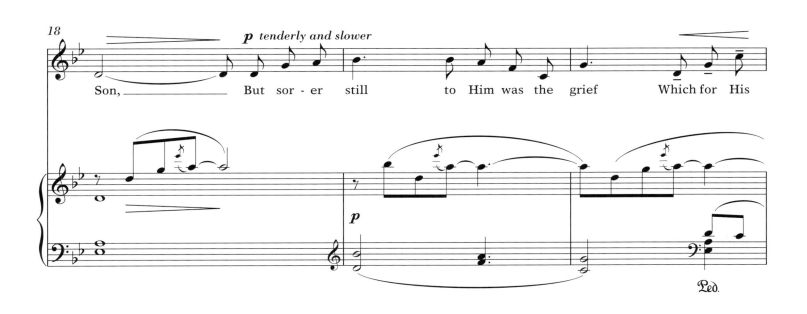

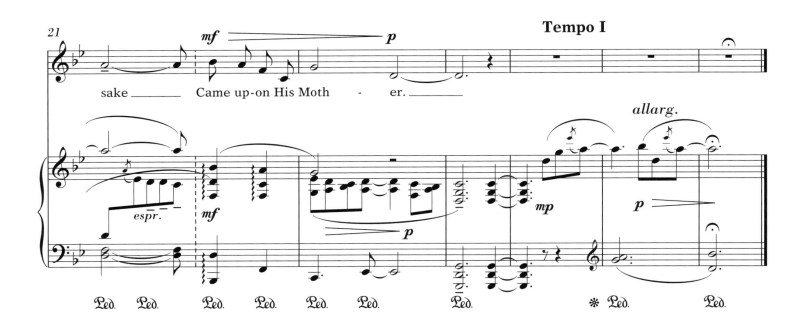

to Daisy

The Daisies
original key: F major

James Stephens*

Samuel Barber
Op. 2, No. 1

*From *Collected Poems of James Stephens*. Printed by permission of The Macmillan Company, publishers.

Hey nonny no!

original key: C major

Anonymous (16th century)

Samuel Barber
(1927)

Mother, I cannot mind my wheel

original key: A minor

Walter Savage Landor

Samuel Barber
(1927)

A Slumber Song of the Madonna

original key: F minor/A–flat major

Alfred Noyes

Samuel Barber
(1925)

Text used by permission.

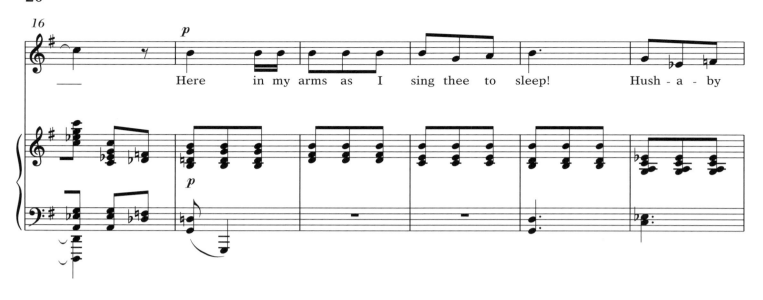

Here in my arms as I sing thee to sleep! Hush - a - by

Poco più mosso

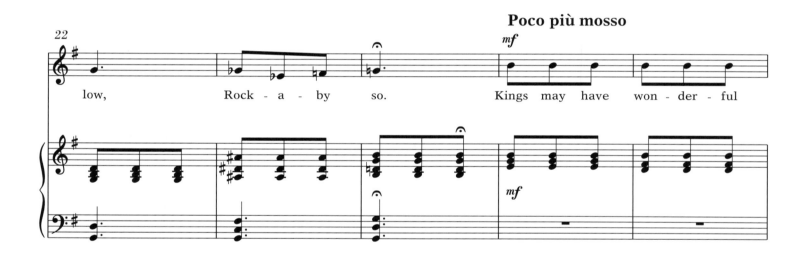

low, Rock - a - by so. Kings may have won - der - ful

jew - els to bring! Moth - er has on - ly a kiss for her

The Secrets of the Old

original key: a minor third higher

W.B. Yeats*

Samuel Barber
Op. 13, No. 2

*The words of this song are reprinted from "COLLECTED POEMS OF W.B. YEATS" by permission of Mrs. Yeats and of the Macmillan Company, Publishers.

And what had drowned a lov - er once Sounds like an __ old __

song. _____ Though Mar - g'ry is strick-en dumb If

thrown in Madge-'s way, We three make up a sol - i-tude;

Strings in the earth and air

original key: C major

James Joyce

Samuel Barber
(1935)

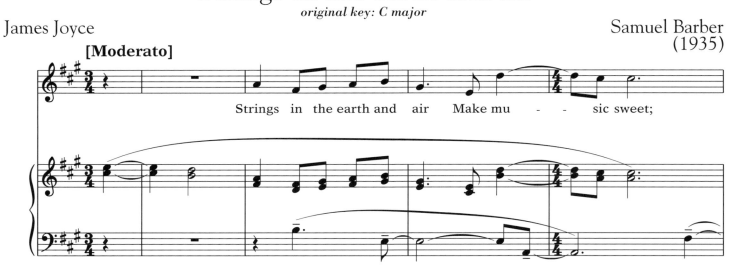

Text used by permission.

All soft - ly play - ing, With

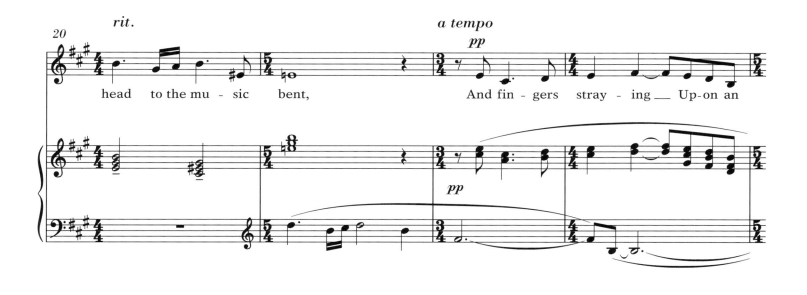

rit. *a tempo*

head to the mu - sic bent, And fin - gers stray - ing __ Up-on an

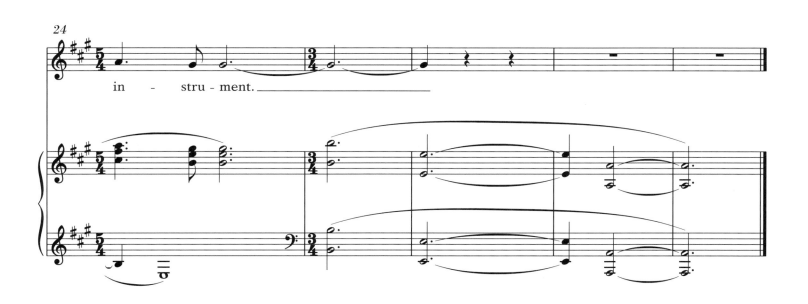

in - stru - ment. _____

to Gama Gilbert

With rue my heart is laden

original key: D minor

A.E. Housman*

Samuel Barber
Op. 2, No. 2

*From "A Shropshire Lad"; words used by permission of the poet and The Richard Press Ltd., publishers.

to Sara

Sure on this shining night

original key: B-flat major

James Agee*

Samuel Barber
Op. 13, No. 3

*From "Permit Me Voyage". Used by permission of Yale University Press, Publishers.

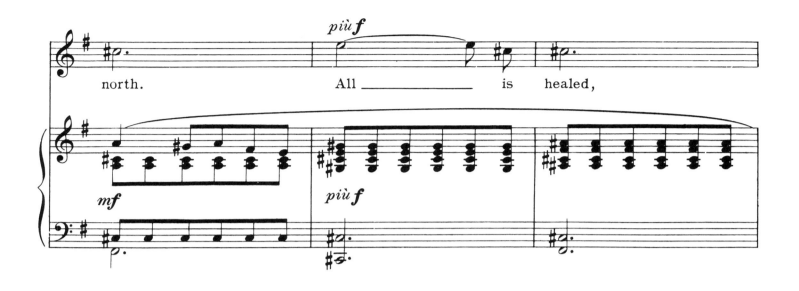

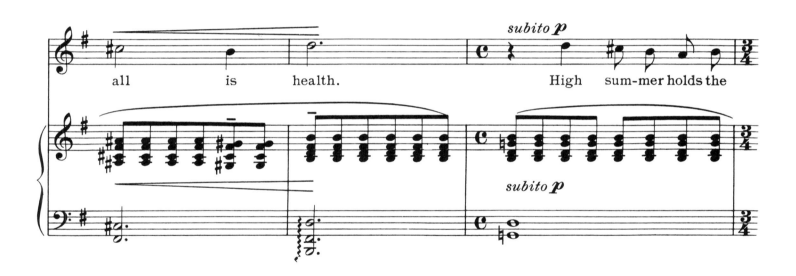